leave **no one** behind

Pursuing the Next Generation With God's Love

Mike Novotny

Published by Straight Talk Books
P.O. Box 301, Milwaukee, WI 53201
800.661.3311 • timeofgrace.org

Printed in the United States of America
ISBN: 978-1-949488-28-9

Contents

Introduction

Last fall my 8-year-old daughter dressed up like an 80-year-old woman. She got on stage with 50 other kids dressed as gray-haired, walker-wielding great-grandparents, and they all sang together: "Kids! I don't know what's wrong with these kids today!" Ever heard that song? It comes from the 1960s musical *Bye Bye Birdie*, but the lyrics are timeless because every generation says the same thing about the generation after it—What happened? If you graduated during the 70s, your hair and bell-bottoms probably drove your grandparents nuts. If you were a child of the 90s, your dad might have vented about your *Street Fighter II* addiction. If you're a millennial, your mom doesn't get why you only talk via text. And if you're under 24, you wonder why anyone would text when you can Snapchat.

Those in that last generation were born between 1995 and 2012. It's the latest generation to get an official name—Generation Z. Generation Z is made up of grade-schoolers, high schoolers, college students, and young adults—24 percent of the American population. Gen Z might be you or your younger sister or your nephew or your son or your neighbor or the person sitting next to you in church on Sunday. In fact, I'd love for you to write down the name of someone from Gen Z whom you know/love.

Like every generation, these "kids" are different. Not better or worse, not good or bad, just different, like you were probably different from your parents. Dr. Jean Twenge, a psychology professor from San Diego State, recently compared Gen Z to the rest of us. While every person is obviously an individual, she noticed a few striking trends among the youngest Americans. They like the *internet*—the average Gen Zer spends six hours on social media, apps, and the internet each day. They sleep within arm's reach of their phones and use them to connect with friends. They're also *independent*. They're much less likely to be a Democrat or a Republican or committed to any Christian denomination. They're *inclusive;* they've seen and read of the damage done to minorities in previous generations and have no plans to repeat the past. Many are *in no hurry* to start "adulting," with fewer high schoolers getting a driver's license and fewer 20-somethings getting married or having kids. Many are also *insecure* (mental health is a massive struggle), anxious about what others think and afraid that they won't make enough money to pay back their immense student loans.[1]

So far, what do you think of Gen Z? Are you fascinated? frustrated? grateful? fearful? One of the biggest dangers for us older folks is pride. Like my 80-year-old daughter sang, "Why can't they be like we were, perfect in every way?" Yeah, right. Jesus warned about this kind of pride, especially among religious people and specifically with kids. **"Do not despise one of these little ones,"** Jesus commanded his disciples (Matthew 18:10).

But there's something else you should know about Gen Z. They are, according to Dr. Twenge's data, *irreligious,* the "least religious generation in US history."[2] One in four high school seniors and one in three college students don't ever go to church, don't ever pray, and don't even believe in God. In my community, from 2000 to

2010 those unaffiliated with any church of any religion grew by 681 percent.[3] I fear the 2020 census will make that number look small.

For many Christians, this is at the top of our prayer lists. We pray for our kids, grandkids, nieces, nephews, younger brothers, classmates, and peers from church. As a church, we think about families and pray for college students. We want the kids to stay close to Jesus and his Word and his people. And, for those who have wandered away, we pray they come back. *We don't want anyone left behind.*

But what if there was something else we could do besides just stay and pray? What if God was calling us to something bigger, more challenging, but more beautiful? Because that's what Jesus taught his disciples to do.

The Next Generation

In Matthew chapter 18, Jesus taught his longest sermon ever about the next generation. "Don't sin against the kids," he insisted. "Don't look down on the kids," he warned. And then Jesus said something famous. It's a short story you might've heard but might not have known that it was, at least in Matthew's gospel, about the next generation.

Check out Jesus' words: **"What do you think? If a man owns a hundred sheep, and one of them wanders away, will he not leave the ninety-nine on the hills and go to look for the one that wandered off?"** (verse 12). What do you think? Jesus wants to know your answer. If you got a 99 percent on your chemistry final, would you think it's a good grade? If you retained 99 percent of your clients from the past year, would you think it's good business? If you ended the day with 99 percent of your flock, would you think it's a good church? If 99 percent of the kids stuck around and 99 percent of the chairs were occupied on Sunday, would that be good? What do you think?

Think of it like this family from my church. Brian and Amanda have five sons: Logan, Parker, Myles, Lincoln, and Sawyer. Can you imagine if they went on vacation and came home with only four sons in the back of the oversized white van they drive? If Logan was lost, would Brian be cool with that? Would Amanda shrug and say, "Well, we still have four. That's more than most families!" What do you think? No! That's not just a stat; that's her son!

That is a sheep the Shepherd can't stand to lose.

And that's how God feels about the Gen Z name you wrote down. The one teenager in your family. The one guy on your team. The one girl from your dorm. That person is a soul God created. That person was someone on Jesus' mind when he went to the cross. That is a person the Spirit is reaching out to. That is a sheep the Shepherd can't stand to lose.

But sometimes sheep wander. We're all prone to wander. Jesus didn't say in this verse that we run away or rebel but that we wander. Like a sheep that sees a good patch of green grass just over there . . . and then another . . . and then . . . we can end up in a place far from the flock, far from the Shepherd. A place we never planned to be.

If you're fairly young, wandering will be one of your greatest temptations. I feel for you because you face some temptations I didn't have to face growing up. Like economic insecurity. College is insanely expensive. So you pack in the AP courses, the college credits, and work weekend shifts to save up. You're not against church, it's just . . . Then there's the internet. You know more of the ugly parts of organized religion than your grandparents. You've read stories of hypocrisy, greed, abuse, cover-up. You're like kids who witnessed a bitter divorce and now are nervous about marriage. You've seen the ugliest parts of church, and I don't blame you for wandering from every-Sunday worship. Then there are your friends, your tribe, your family. They're probably way more diverse—ethnically, spiritually, sexually—than Grandma's friends. There are so many ways to wander. I don't want you to. God doesn't either. But I get it. I get why it happens.

So, what will the rest of us do when it happens? When that name you wrote down is working and not here worshiping. When she has a bad experience and votes spiritually independent. When they start caring more for how their friends feel than for what their Father feels, what will we do? Just complain about the kids? Just stay and pray? Just wish they wouldn't wander?

No, listen again to Jesus: **"Will he not leave the ninety-nine on the hills and go to look for the one that wandered off?"** The Good Shepherd doesn't stay and pray. He goes and gets. He leaves and looks. Picture him at the end of a hard day. The sun is going down. The sheep are lying down in the pen. "97, 98," the Shepherd counts. "99 . . . wait." He counts again. Then again. He squints out at the field, looking for a patch of white wool. Nothing. So, what does he do? He leaves. He looks. It'll be work. He doesn't have an F-150 with heated seats. He'll go down into the valley, climb up the mountain, plunge into the shadows ready to fight any wolf that took away his one. That's what love does. Love looks. Love goes and gets.

I won't lie to you. Finding wanderers and turning them into worshipers will not be easy. Things have changed. The cultural ideas that "I really should get back to church" and "Church is a good thing" and "Christians are admirable people" are dead. When people find out I'm a Christian pastor,

That's what love does. Love looks. Love goes and gets.

they're not impressed; they feel awkward. The internet and TV have taught them what people like me are like: money-hungry hypocrites who cheat on their wives, hate gay people and immigrants, and have sworn a blood oath to the Republican Party. So, it takes time, lots of time, to prove them wrong, to go and get them to change their minds. It takes a lot of listening, a lot of love. It takes years of building trust, of opening a door. This will take time. We can't squeeze going and getting into those small slots in our schedules. It might take years of showing how Jesus does make a difference in life and in suffering and in pain. We can't hide, and we can't hate. We have to go and get. Not with some evangelistic agenda. But with the goal to show them God's love.

So, what would looking be like for you? What would love do? In the rest of this book, I want to speak to fathers and mothers and the entire Christian family about that love, but maybe today you could start by thinking about what looking would be like. What would be the best way to show your love to that one? What would you say? What would you do? When would you talk? How could you connect? In an anxious generation, how could they see, up close and personal, the power of knowing the God who's got it? How could you let your light shine?

Because something amazing might happen: **"And if he finds it** [the Good Shepherd finds his wandering one]**, truly I tell you, he is happier about that one sheep than about the ninety-nine that did not wander off"** (Matthew 18:13). Happy. That's how he feels. Insanely happy. How else could you feel when someone who matters so much gets found?

That's how I feel about Lacey. Lacey is a young woman who came to my church a year ago and said I could share her story. Lacey had some spiritual connections growing up, but life got busy and she wandered. She didn't really know Jesus or trust in God's power. But now you should see her. Lacey has her roots deep into Jesus. She gathers with us on Sundays and does life in a small Bible study group and grows in the Word at home and gives generously and goes to let her light shine. And she has spiritual fruit. More peace than in the past. More love for her family. More joy because of Jesus. And that makes me so happy. You make me happy, you 99 who haven't wandered, but there's something so good about the 1.

What if this year, your "one" became the next Lacey? Could you imagine that for a moment? What if a year from now that person was in church with you? What if you heard that person's voice joining yours in the Lord's Prayer? What if you saw that person's progress on the Bible app and liked his or her highlighted passage with the happiest emoji face you could find?

What if he got baptized? What if she came back to Jesus?

What if he got baptized? What if she came back to Jesus? That could actually happen. That has happened. That does happen when we love and look, when we go and get.

Like Jesus did with us. He concludes in Matthew chapter 18, **"In the same way your Father in heaven is not willing that any of these little ones should perish"** (verse 14). In the same way, just like that shepherd would go and get the one, God did too. He wasn't cool with 99 Christians. He cared about the wandering one. He cared about you. You were not some number on God's spreadsheet. You were a name, a name he knew, a face he couldn't stand not to see. That's why Jesus didn't stay and pray in heaven. No, he loved enough to come look. He left heaven, he lived perfectly, and then left the tomb empty. Jesus loved you enough to die for you, to forgive you, to invite you. And he loved you enough to nudge your mom or your brother or your boyfriend or your best friend to love you, to invite you, to tell you about God's unconditional love. Because God is love. Because that Love looked.

That's what musician Cory Asbury figured out. Cory was not a Christian as a kid. Raised by a far-from-perfect father, he struggled to understand what God the Father was like. Probably angry at him. Disappointed. Distant. But in 2010, something changed because Cory had a son. When he held his baby in his arms, he felt a love like nothing he had felt before. An overwhelming feeling. And he realized that his kid hadn't done anything, hadn't earned it, hadn't deserved it, but he still felt it. He finally understood the Father's heart. The heart that would do anything—climb a mountain, kick down a wall, plunge himself into the darkness, risk it all—for the sake of just one. So, one day, Cory Asbury picked up a pen and wrote a song you might have heard: "Reckless Love." It's all about the overwhelming, unending, reckless love that God has for us. We don't deserve it, but he gives it to us freely. When Cory wrote the song, some Christians wondered if *reckless* was the right word to describe God's love, but what other word would describe a Shepherd who would sacrifice his safety, his comfort, his life? Who would lay down everything for the sake of just one who wandered?

Christians, this is our story. We wandered, and Jesus found us. And it made him so happy that the angels threw a party. That's the story we want for the next generation. To be overwhelmed by the reckless love of Jesus and the Father's gracious heart. So, let's go and get. Let's look. Let's love so another generation would love our Savior Jesus.

.

Study Guide

1. When we think of the next generation, we often fall into the trap of pride in our own and disdain for the younger. Proverbs 11:2 says, "When pride comes, then comes disgrace, but with humility comes wisdom." How does a prideful mind-set get in the way of actions that you can take in humility and wisdom?

    _____

    _____

    _____

    _____

    _____

    _____

    _____

    _____

    _____

2. Write down the name of one person you know in Generation Z. Now look at Matthew 18:12-14 again. With that name on your paper in mind, explain how 99 percent can seem like a failing grade.

_____

_____

_____

_____

_____

_____

_____

_____

_____

_____

_____

3. Being compared to sheep is not entirely complimentary, but when you look at it in the proper context, you can rejoice that you're one of Jesus' flock. John chapter 10 is often called the Good Shepherd chapter. Read through verses 1-18. How does Jesus' striking statement in verse 10 shed light on his purpose as our Shepherd? What sort of relationship between sheep and Shepherd is highlighted in verse 14?

_____

_____

_____

_____

_____

_____

_____

_____

_____

4. And yet, wandering happens. We might wander; those we love might wander. And then what? Jesus tells us what: He goes and gets. He left heaven to look for us. Love takes action. Dig into James 2:15-17, which speaks to putting our faith into action. Aside from prayer, what sorts of actions can you take to help those who are wandering? (*Warning: This might not be a quick fix—this might be long-term measures and time-consuming relationship building. This is not for the faint of heart, but that name on your paper is a soul worth every ounce of effort.)

_____

_____

_____

_____

_____

_____

_____

Prayer

Dear Jesus, my Good Shepherd, I come before you with your precious sheep on my mind and heart. I know you care for them as you care for me. You've called them by name, and you laid down your life for them as you did for me. Thank you for leading me to you and for the special relationship that I'm blessed to have with you as my Shepherd. Lord, I want that for the next generation, for those whose names I know and for those whose names you know and whom you've called. Help me take action to go and get, in humility and wisdom; help me guide souls back to you so that I may rejoice with you whenever a sheep is found because of your reckless love. In your name I pray. Amen.

Journal

1. What has caused you to wander in the past? What (or who) has helped to bring you back from being a wanderer and kept you as a worshiper? Are there "wandering triggers" that you've learned to avoid or gentle tugs from the Good Shepherd that you've felt?

_____

_____

_____

_____

_____

_____

_____

_____

_____

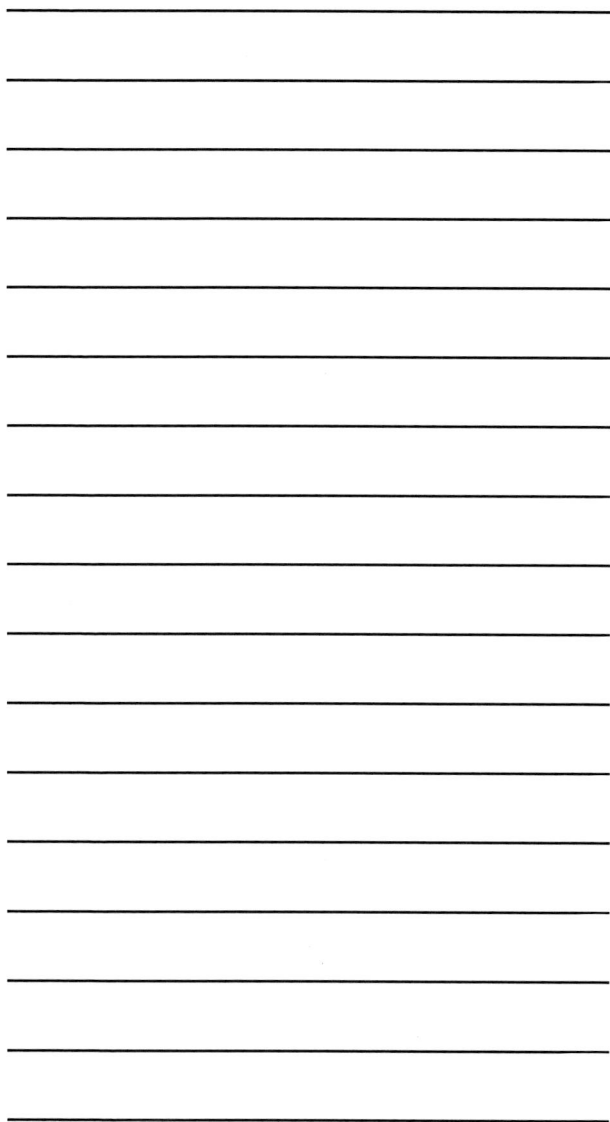

2. Isaiah 43:1 contains a mighty promise from the Lord. He has called you by name, and you are his. How does this turn you from just a "stat" into a son (or daughter) of the Lord, and why does that "naming" make such a huge difference?

_____

_____

_____

_____

_____

_____

_____

_____

_____

_____

Start Young

In my office, I keep a picture of the next generation. It's a picture of a member of Gen Z, those born from 1995 to 2012, whom I care a little bit about. It's a picture of my daughter Brooklyn from when she was two. I really want this girl to know GOD, to know she's loved by GOD, to trust GOD, to follow GOD. And so far, so good. She comes to church every Sunday. She reads the Bible and prays and sings to Jesus at home. But . . . she's 10. And I know when she's 20, it won't be so simple. She's going to have her own car, her own schedule, her own life, her own choices. And there's no guarantee she'll believe in Jesus like I do. There's nothing I want more in the universe than to have my kids love Jesus. There's nothing that scares me more than that they won't.

Do you love someone like this? Someone from the next generation? Maybe your best friend, your teammate, your son, your nephew, your granddaughter, or the teens you see at church? Could you pick one whom you care about? Could you close your eyes for a moment and picture that person's face? Imagine, in ten years, where he or she will be. Imagine what that person will believe.

Whoever it was, I bet you want what's best for that kid. And if you're a Christian, I bet your definition of *best* is like mine. You want them to know Jesus. To know Jesus' love so personally that they love him with everything they've got. You want them to one day seek GOD and find security, to know GOD and his true identity, to love GOD and his entire family. That's what Christians want for the next generation.

So, what's the best way to help that happen? No, we can't make anyone believe anything, but we can do something. As parents, siblings, friends, family, fellow Christians, we can do something. So what somethings should we do? That question has never been so debated as the last 50 years in America. How do we keep kids connected to Christ? There have been lots of answers. Sunday schools and Christian schools. Youth pastors and youth groups. Screens for their visual minds. Bands for their musical tastes. Children's church so they can have fun and hear a tailor-made message. Churches wrestle hard with this issue. We spend crazy hours and crazy dollars because we care about the kids. We care more than anything about the faith of the church's children.

> More than ever, teens and young adults don't pray ... don't believe in God.

But can I tell you some hard news? It's not going well. More than ever, teens and young adults don't pray, don't do church, don't believe in God. Even with the programs, the music, the Christian education, Generation Z is the least religious generation in American history. The numbers are scary, especially when they're personal, when you know their names and can see their faces.

So, what should we do? Just hope and pray that our person is the exception to the rule? Just try not to think about it on the way to basketball practice? Or ... what if there was something else? Something a bit more ... biblical? Because the Bible has a lot to say about the next generation, but it's not about programs or events or even pastors or teachers. Those things aren't bad; they're just far from the best. I want to show you God's best way to keep the next generation close to Christ, a path that even modern data supports as the most effective way to keep the faith alive and well in our culture.

Check out this classic passage from Proverbs 22: **"Train up a child in the way he should go, and when he is old he will not turn from it"** (verse 6 NIV84). From the earliest years, God wants us to train our children. Not to wait until later, but to start right now. That doesn't guarantee a godly life, but the proverb tells you what's probable—they will not turn from it.

Think of that word—*train*. Why do you train for something? Train for a 5k? Train for the start of the season? Because to succeed then, you have to do something now. If you don't train now, you won't run the 5k well then. If you want to win, to conquer, to celebrate then, it's essential to train now. And that's true with children. Every psychologist and educator knows the importance of the early years. Of the little kids receiving love, affection, and reading time in Mommy's

God wants us to train our children.

lap. To succeed in school and in life then, parents start "training" now. We don't worry about stuffing books or nutritious foods down their throats. As adults, we know what's good for them. So, we train them up. We start them off. According to this passage, the same applies to their spiritual lives.

Think of it like a baton. Imagine the baton is Jesus and you really want to pass Jesus to the next generation. When they're little, they're right there, sitting on the floor. Here you go! Then they crawl, but you can still catch them. Here you go! They learn to walk, but they can't outrun you. During the early years, you can stay close. Ah, but what happens during the teenage years? They outrun you. You're getting slower, and they're running faster. A gap grows in your influence, your quantity time, your connection. And so the best time to pass on the faith is when they're young.

We can do this with a simple and repeated question: "Isn't GOD _____?" That's a great way to train up a child. To connect the stuff of everyday life to the qualities of GOD that we love. During a big Saturday breakfast with sausage and pancakes, "Isn't GOD good? He let these gifts to us be blessed." During a day at the pool, "Isn't GOD smart? He thought of water, the hydrogen and oxygen and the look of it."

Just talk about GOD. "Isn't GOD generous? The car started, the sun came up, our friends came over." "Isn't GOD forgiving? We didn't do it right today, but Jesus died for us." You don't have to be a Bible expert to train up a child. Just talk about GOD. You don't need a church or even a set devotional time. Just talk about GOD. That's how you train up a child.

But it turns out that not all "trainers" are the same. While we all have a role in that training, God has a sacred calling for a few of you reading this book.

Paul shares that calling in Ephesians 6:4: **"Fathers, do not exasperate your children; instead, bring them up in the training and instruction of the Lord."** Fathers. Paul wants a word with the dads. Quick heads-up—next chapter, God is going to talk to the rest of us—to mothers, brothers, pastors, friends, church family. But in this passage, Paul wants to talk about the explosive impact of a father's faith. Maybe you've read the studies for yourself. Nothing makes a bigger difference statistically as a dad who trains spiritually. A dad who brings the kids to church. A dad who prays out loud in front of his daughter. A dad who talks to his son about Jesus.

But before Paul gets to that training, he has a warning: **"Fathers, do not exasperate your children."** Sounds bad, doesn't it? Exasperate. It is. To exasperate means to infuriate, to irritate, to provoke your kids to anger. Obviously, not every angry kid is evidence of a bad dad, but Paul knows that religious fathers can be the worst. They can wreck a child's view of religion, of faith, of God.

Dads, I thought of three dangerous ways for us to exasperate our kids. Three sins where our Father says, "Don't!" Write these down please. First—*hypocrisy*. When you're a different man at church than you are at home. When you sing at church and shout at home. When you shake hands at church and shake fists at home. When you fake being faithful, you sabotage the faith of your children. You don't have to be perfect to go to church, but you need to be real. If you're a controlling man, an angry man, a selfish man, a drunk man, you need to tell your church friends. If I ask you how you are and you lie to me, your kids will think church is for liars. If you want to impress someone, don't impress other church members. Impress that someone. Don't be a hypocrite. Don't fake it. Be real. That's real religion.

Second—*no love*. The next generation knows what so many of us forgot—love. Love matters to Jesus. Love for your enemies matters to Jesus. Love for immigrants, for Democrats and Republicans, for straight and transgender matters to Jesus. You don't have to agree with everyone, but you are called to love everyone. So, if you claim to know Jesus but go home and hate your neighbor, your kids might hate Jesus. If you grumble about "those people" and become a crotchety old Christian, you will corrupt the magnetic message of Christianity, a God who loved his enemies so much he died for them. Watch your words, dads.

Third—*all law*. Christian fathers rightly care about God's laws. They discipline their kids based on God's definition of good and bad. And that's good. But it's bad if that's all kids hear. Have you ever worked for a boss you could never make happy? His standard of excellence was so high your best was never good enough? That can happen with religion too. As fathers, we can't miss the main point of Jesus' message: the gospel. The love of God. The forgiveness of sins. Jesus has a PhD in mercy, in compassion, in grace. High standards aren't bad, but they are a burden without the gospel.

"Fathers, do not exasperate your children; instead, bring them up in the training and instruction of the Lord." Dads, here's the good part. Here's the best way to train up a child. Bring your kids up to know the Lord Jesus.

A few years ago, I heard a pastor and his son speak at a men's conference. The son told the story of when he got his fiancée pregnant, a fact he was scared to tell his very religious parents. When he finally got the courage and shared the news, his fiancée burst out crying. The pastor and his wife looked at each other, and they knew exactly what to do. Mom embraced her future daughter-in-law with a hug full of Christian love. Pastor Dad told his son he loved him, told him about forgiveness, told him about Jesus. Months later, at the wedding, the father of the bride, a non-Christian man, expected the church folks would show up with crossed arms and scowling judgment. But he experienced something else: people who had been trained and instructed by grace. The grace of our Lord Jesus Christ.

"Fathers . . . bring them up in the training and instruction of the Lord." Yes, our sons and daughters need strong values, a good moral compass, discipline that gets them ready to run the race of faith. But they need grace even more. After they hit their mommies in a tantrum, they need grace. After they throw a fit and feel bad, they need grace. After they search for something online they shouldn't or lie about what really happened, they need grace. When they get mocked on social media or dumped after third hour or left out of the invite list, they need a Savior who still chooses, still wants, and still loves them. They need a grace so deep it gets down to their deepest secrets. A grace so wide it covers their biggest messes. A grace so high they will never outgrow it. In Ephesians 1:11, Paul says, **"In** [Jesus] **we were also chosen."** In chapter 2, he writes, **"It is by grace you have been saved"** (verse 8). A chapter later, he says, **"We may approach God with freedom and confidence"** (3:12). **"God forgave you,"** Paul promises in Ephesians 4:32. **"Christ . . . gave himself up for us,"** Paul insists in Ephesians 5:2. And then Paul gets to Ephesians 6:4: "Dads, bring them up in that. Train them in that. Raise them with the grace of Jesus."

Guys, this is the most important thing we will ever do. No CEO salary or NFL contract could compare to this. This is our calling. When we lie dying, our bosses and clients will barely remember us. But our children will never forget us. Let's use the little time we have to pass the baton of the best thing in the world—the grace of God. And for all of you who aren't dads, we dads need you. We really do. We need guy friends to grab us by the face mask and snap us out of worldly thinking. We need you to remind us that there are a thousand people who could do our jobs but only one man on earth who can be their dad. We need our friend groups to ask God for wisdom so we know what to do and when and how. We need you to ask us what we're doing to train them up. We need you to help us do it.

Most important, we need you to remind us of our Father, that our Father in heaven forgives fathers on earth. That he doesn't remember our sins, even the sins against our kids. That he promises to send his Spirit when we ask for help. That the God of the universe drives home with us, walks through that door with us, and swears he will help us. That's what we need. We need God, just like our kids.

They grow up so fast, don't they? My two-year-old from the picture in my office is now a ten-ager (that's what she told me on her birthday). I think I'm two blinks away from her turning 20. But I have hope. Hope that God can hold on to our kids. Hope that he can do far beyond what we expect or imagine. So, let's pray for that. That we would train up our children in the way they should go, so that when they are old, they listen to Jesus, know they're loved by Jesus, and lead the next generation to Jesus.

Study Guide

1. Solomon writes in Proverbs 22:6, "Train up a child in the way he should go, and when he is old he will not turn from it." A different and perhaps stronger translation for that word *train* is "dedicate," which is a word used earlier in the Bible when King Solomon dedicated the temple he built to the Lord. How does that translation portray a greater commitment and active devotion to this duty you are given as a parent or caregiver?

_____

_____

_____

_____

_____

_____

2. Read 2 Timothy 3:14-17. How does this section give you even more guidance as you train up your children in the way they should go? What does it mean and why is it important that the Scripture you are training them up in is "God-breathed"?

_____

_____

_____

_____

_____

_____

_____

_____

_____

_____

3. A special exhortation is given to fathers in Ephesians 6:4, and the apostle Paul takes it a step further in his writings to the Colossians, saying, "Fathers, do not embitter your children, or they will become discouraged" (3:21). Why does God call out fathers specifically in these verses? How might children become "discouraged," "embittered," and "exasperated," and what can that lead to later in their lives?

_____

_____

_____

_____

_____

_____

_____

_____

_____

4. Now let's back up a bit in the book of Colossians. Read Colossians 3:12-17. How do these verses speak hope and life into Christian households and families? Why is grace and forgiveness so important in a family? Why is it vital to admit your own wrongdoings and ask your children for forgiveness as well as modeling grace and forgiveness to them?

_____

_____

_____

_____

_____

_____

_____

_____

_____

Prayer

Heavenly Father, you've been the perfect trainer. You've modeled grace and forgiveness and have shown me how to love and train up my children to know you. You have given me your Word that I can use to breathe life and love into my children. You have also given me a high calling and responsibility in my household and church. Be with me as I muddle through the adventure of parenting and training. Forgive me when I make a mess of things, and teach me to ask my own kids humbly for forgiveness when necessary, so they too may learn how to show grace and love. Hang on tightly to my kids, to that next generation, Jesus. In your name. Amen.

Journal

1. Aside from teaching kids to know Jesus and his love, we are all called to teach them how to defend their faith when they are faced with questions from the big wide world. Check out 1 Peter 3:15. What is the reason for the hope that you have? How can you start preparing your kids to be confident in that hope and use their God-given logic to defend the Bible and its truths?

   _____

   _____

   _____

   _____

   _____

   _____

   _____

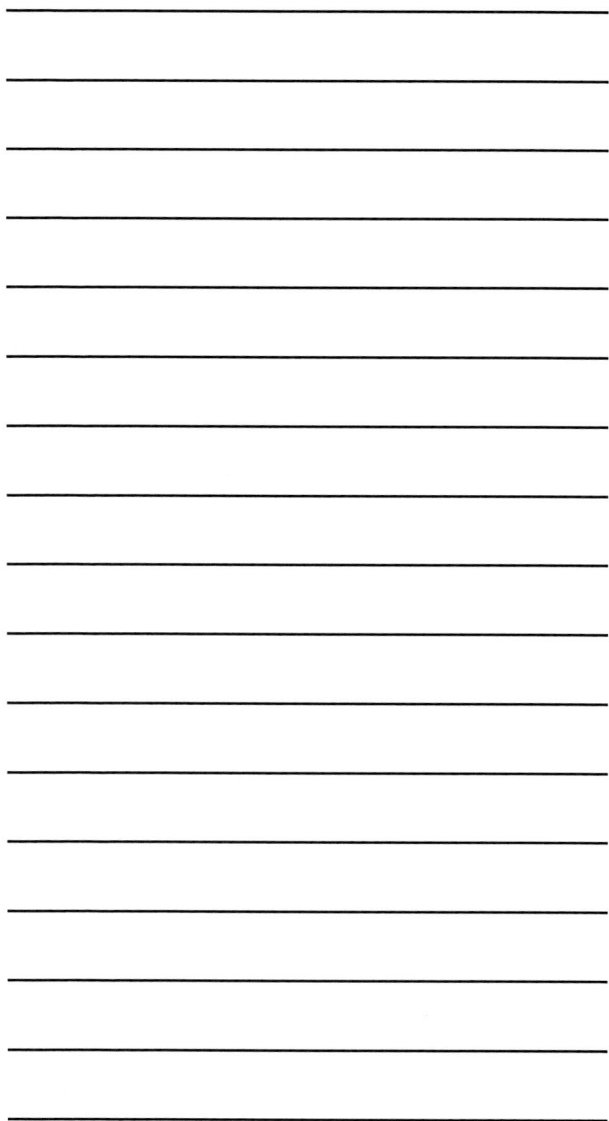

2. If you train for a marathon, there's still no guarantee you'll finish the race, but you trust the training and know that the foundation has been laid for the best chance of success. If you train up your children in the way they should go, you don't have a guarantee that your children will not stray from God, but you trust that the foundation has been laid and you have hope that God holds on tightly to your kids. Ephesians 3:20,21 assures you, "Now to him who is able to do immeasurable more than all we ask or imagine, according to his power that is at work within us, to him be glory in the church and in Christ Jesus throughout all generations, for ever and ever!" Write about times when you trained for something and it paid off. Or write about a time when you asked God for something and he gave you more than you ever asked for or imagined.

_____

_____

_____

Embrace Your Role

Class of 2021. That's what her T-shirt said. My quiet afternoon in the Y weight room turned into a swarm of high school and college kids, one whose T-shirt reminded me how old I am—Class of 2021?! I was old enough to vote when she was born. Among the dozens of us in the gym, I and one other couple were the only people not from Generation Z. Have you ever been in a situation like that? No matter what your age or generation, I hope you think of Jesus' words when you think about them: **"Your Father in heaven is not willing that any of these little ones should perish"** (Matthew 18:14). Despite all the differences between us— the age, the experiences, the music, the life-styles—God is not willing to lose a single soul from the next generation. God loved everyone so much that he sent Jesus. Jesus loved everyone so much that he gave up everything and died. The Holy Spirit loves everyone so much that he's reaching, leading, trying to bring them all to Jesus.

If you finished the last chapter, you know the best way, scripturally and statistically, to get the next generation passionate about Jesus—Fathers. God uses Fathers to raise the next generation. When dads train up their children and bring them up to know the grace of Jesus, there's nothing like it. When dads don't just have a business plan or financial goals but a Jesus plan and faith goals for their kids, watch out! If fathers tell their sons and daughters who they are (loved by God) and why they're here (to show God's love), it's revival time!

But . . . there's a problem. Even if you believe everything I just wrote, there's a problem. Even if you care about the next generation like our Father and even if you pray for faithful fathers, there's a problem. The problem is . . . not every kid has a godly dad. And we can't change that. We can't take all the kids and squeeze them into the homes of a few good men. They wouldn't fit. We can't rewind and give dads a do-over. We are where we are. It is what it is.

Which can feel discouraging. According to Dr. Jean Twenge, the number of college students whose parents have no religion increased from 5 percent in the late 70s to 17 percent by 2016.[4] And if this generation continues the trend, the number of souls who will grow up without a dad who loves Jesus, without much Jesus at all, is staggering.

But before we lose hope, we need to read the book of Acts. Acts tracks the Christian church from about A.D. 30 to A.D. 60 when Christians went from this tiny minority of 120 people to a massive movement that changed the world. And here's what I want you to know about the book: that explosive growth happened in all kinds of ways. Not just dads raising kids with Bible stories. But with moms, grandmas, pastors, neighbors, strangers, friends, sorcerers (yeah, we'll get to them!), all kinds of people. In other words, when Christianity exploded, people like you changed the next generation. I want to show you three stories from the **People like you changed the next generation.** book of Acts to stir your passion for your classmates, your coworkers, and your friends from the next generation.

The first story is about Paul. Paul was originally known as Saul and he is, perhaps, the most famous Christian ever. But Paul wasn't raised with Jesus. In fact, most of his life was anti-Jesus. He was very religious and very convinced Jesus was very wrong. Paul was like the university professor who murdered Christians in public debates. Actually, Paul even murdered Christians (period).

But then something happened. Paul was marching up to Damascus in Syria ready to arrest more of Jesus' people when something happened, something Paul spent the rest of his life trying to explain. He experienced something—a bright light, a voice from heaven, an encounter with Jesus. And it rocked him. For days, Paul hid himself away in a rented room. He prayed. He tried to process what happened. And then Ananias showed up. You know Ananias? No? That's the point. He was just a Christian who happened to live in Damascus. And he was the guy God sent to talk to Paul. The one who, honestly, was terrified to go. But he went. And he talked about Jesus. And Paul changed. **"In Damascus there was a disciple named Ananias. The Lord called to him in a vi-**

sion, 'Ananias!' 'Yes, Lord,' he answered. The Lord told him, 'Go to the house of Judas on Straight Street and ask for a man from Tarsus named Saul, for he is praying'" (Acts 9:10,11).

What's the point? God uses neighbors to reach the next generation. People who just happen to live next door or work next door or have the locker next door. Do you have any Gen Zers living next door, maybe some who aren't so sure about God? Your 18-year-old nephew who is very public about his atheism. Your friend who says she only believes in science and wants nothing to do with Jesus. Your new neighbors whose views are so different than what you grew up with. The people you think, "That'll never happen." Which is what Ananias said, but he couldn't have known what God was up to.

And God might be up to something with your "Pauls" too. Maybe not a bright light or a voice from heaven. Maybe it's more like a tragedy in life—a divorce they didn't see coming, a death no one expected, a depression they can't shake. Maybe it's the nagging feeling that there's got to be something more than paying off school loans, paying the bills, and paying for a funeral. Maybe they fall in love with you. Maybe they have their first kid. Maybe they read the Bible to mock it and it moves them. Maybe something happens they never expected. And maybe God will send you to connect the dots.

Maybe God will send you to connect the dots.

Like that Methodist minister who shared Jesus with Francis Collins. Collins was a confident atheist with a degree in quantum mechanics from Yale and a budding medical career that would eventually lead him to head up the Human Genome Research Institute. But during his residency, Collins noticed something—the way Christians suffered. Despite the pain in their bodies, they still prayed to God, leaned on God, loved God. And Collins realized that, although he had studied so many fields so deeply, he had never dug into the roots of their faith. So, at age 27, he went to see a Methodist pastor. The pastor listened to his views, his accusations about religion, his assumptions about Jesus, and then gently suggested he read the Bible and the works of another former atheist scholar, C. S. Lewis. So, Collins did. And the rest, you could say, is Christian history. Collins came to see the reason behind the Christian faith, not just in some generic creator but in a personal GOD who loved and forgave him.

Do you know the name of that Methodist minister? I don't either. But, like Ananias, he just so happened to be in the same place as the guy God was working on. And you might be too. So, keep loving well. The atheist, the irreligious, the not-a-church-guy guys. Maybe God will surprise you when they have a question, a doubt, a need. Maybe God will pull another Paul and you'll be another Ananias.

That's the first story. Here's the second—Timothy. Like Paul, Timothy is kind of famous in the Christian faith. Two of the twenty-seven New Testament books have his name in them—1 and 2 Timothy. He was a bold missionary who ended up pastoring the church in Ephesus, a metropolitan community that became a big part of first-century Christianity.

But guess what? Like Paul, Timothy didn't have a Christian dad. Paul explains where that kind of faith came from: **"I am reminded of your sincere faith, which first lived in your**

grandmother Lois and in your mother Eunice and, I am persuaded, now lives in you also" (2 Timothy 1:5). Lois and Eunice. That's where Timothy learned about Jesus. The point? God uses mothers to reach the next generation.

Ladies, what a passage for you. For you moms and grandmas, sisters and aunts, girlfriends and godmothers. Sincere faith, powerful faith, people-talking-about-it faith can come from a few good . . . women. Yes, the next generation will need some godly men too, like Paul was for Timothy, but never let the dad stats discourage you. Maybe, like Eunice, you married a guy who doesn't believe just yet. Maybe you had a kid with an old boyfriend and it's complicated. Maybe your home isn't a picture-perfect spiritual situation. But remember that without these women, your New Testament might only have 25 books. Because if it wasn't for Lois and Eunice, there might not have been a Timothy to write to.

This reminds me of a hallway. . . . It's a hallway that I remember from my childhood that leads to the boys' bathroom at the church where I grew up. I know that hallway well, because every Sunday for over a decade I would walk it while my pastor preached. I always "needed" a bathroom break right about when the pastor started talking, and I would meander from one tile to the next. I'd sit in the stall, even if I was only going #1, and count the little grayish blue bathroom tiles on the floor. And I'd mosey back to Mom ten minutes later. But do you know what happened in that place? I heard about Jesus. And eventually I got excited. I studied the Bible at home. And one day I stumbled across the passage that made me want to become a pastor. These days, I'm so blessed to have my wife and kids and mom and dad and mother-in-law in my church. But back then it was Mom dragging my lazy bones out of bed. I didn't have a Lois and Eunice. Just a Judy.

Moms, don't lose heart. Keep doing what's right. Even if the kids don't get it yet. Grandmas and aunts, don't be discouraged by the dragging feet and the bathroom breaks. Bring them to church. Let them hear. Maybe one day something will click. And their "Do I have to?" will become "I really want to." Maybe they'll end up telling others about Jesus.

That's the second story. Here's the third—Artemis of the Ephesians, the Greek goddess of the hunt. Her towering temple in Ephesus was one of the seven wonders of the ancient world. When Paul dared to say that Jesus was God and Artemis was made up, Ephesus exploded. Tens of thousands flooded into the Ephesian stadium and defended their goddess and demanded Paul's blood. If apple pie is American, then Artemis is Ephesian.

And yet a church started there. One that worshiped Jesus. There were few, if any, Christian dads around. And yet the church grew. The Word spread. The name of Jesus was known. What happened? Crazy stuff like this: **"Many of those who believed now came and openly confessed what they had done. A number who had practiced sorcery brought their scrolls together and burned them publicly. When they calculated the value of the scrolls, the total came to fifty thousand drachmas. In this way the word of the Lord spread widely and grew in power"** (Acts 19:18-20). How great is that?! The sorcerers had a scroll burning. They lit up 50,000 drachmas worth of spells, which is like

$8.6 million! And they openly confessed what they had done. The sorcerers got saved and confessed their sins. God uses *sinners* to reach the next generation.

Now, I don't know too many sorcerers who come to my church, but I do know this: Tons of

God uses sinners to reach the next generation.

people come with stories like that. I think a quarter of my church family has struggled with alcohol, meth, porn, pills, whatever. We come to church before AA or NA or after we get out of jail. And we openly confess what we've done. We don't fake it. We don't put on masks. We confess our sins to one another. We let the other sinners in town know the doors are open and unlocked. We try to be real, relational. And the word about Jesus spreads.

You might think your sin stops you from going, disqualifies you from inviting. Not a chance. We live in a time when people are aching, hurting, searching, turning to all the wrong places, needing something better. Someone better. And your story proves that there is. We who confess our sin prove that Jesus saves by grace and not by works. We prove that getting right with God is about what Jesus has done and not what we have done. Our stories show *God loves his enemies.* that forgiveness is a gift, received by faith, that God loves his enemies, that his goodness is bigger than our badness, that even the worst sinner can become a son of God. And when other sinners hear that, they start to listen.

Put all the stories together and what do you get? Embrace your role in this. It takes a village to raise a church. To raise the next generation we need more than good dads. We need Ananias and Eunice and a couple of sorcerers. We need strangers and mothers and honest confessors. We need you. We need you to embrace your role so no one is left behind.

That's what my church taught me. The other day I opened up my file of all the guests who have come to my church in recent months, all the names I pray for and help connect to Jesus. I thought about how they got there, to that place, to hear about this Jesus. Her husband invited her. His girlfriend brought him. Her parents asked her. His grandmother urged him. They came because of another addict. They came because of a friend. He came because of his boss. She came because of her neighbor. And I realized that there is no one way God reaches the next generation. In his creative love, he uses the whole village. We all have our roles. That's what it takes to reach the next generation.

Study Guide

1. Take a closer look at Saul's conversion into the apostle Paul in Acts 9:1-19. You'll also meet Ananias, the one whom the Lord sent to restore Saul's sight and welcome him as Paul into God's kingdom of believers. Why did God choose Ananias for this job instead of one of Jesus' disciples or known followers? Also, note what Ananias calls Saul in verse 17. How does this simple word show God's grace and forgiveness, and how does it teach you to show the same to your brothers and sisters in Christ?

_____

_____

_____

_____

_____

_____

2. Look up 2 Timothy 1:5-12. God used a few good women to bring Timothy to faith; how did God then use Timothy to "fan into flame the gift of God"? How can this example give you a "spirit of power" to tell others about Jesus, even if you feel timid? What other comfort and encouragement do you receive from these verses?

_____

_____

_____

_____

_____

_____

_____

_____

_____

3. Read through the story of Paul's time in Ephesus. You'll find it in Acts chapter 19. Verse 20 says, "In this way the Word of the Lord spread widely and grew in power." But take note of the time frames throughout this chapter—this did not happen overnight, but over the course of a couple years. How does this give you hope even when it seems like you're not getting through to people with God's Word? What promise does God give you in Isaiah 55:11?

_____

_____

_____

_____

_____

_____

_____

_____

4. Read Romans 10:14,15. How are these passages relevant to the study of "raising a church"? Think about your mission field—where can you live your faith and tell others about Jesus, even without being sent to a foreign land?

_____

_____

_____

_____

_____

_____

_____

_____

_____

_____

Prayer

Dear Jesus, you are so amazing. In your wisdom you give us opportunities all the time to use our strengths and even our weaknesses to reach your village and guide people to you. Help me to build relationships with others, to let down my guard and be real with them and form connections. Help me to be patient, not to give up and to spend the time it takes, because you promise that your Word will not return to you empty. Thank you for those people you sent into my life to be witnesses for you, people who brought me to church or showed me your love in very real ways. Thank you for your Word and for your grace. In your name I pray. Amen.

Journal

1. "There is no one way God reaches the next generation. In his creative love, he uses the whole village." Explore how God used sinful people (like Moses, David, and Paul) to spread his Word, and how God can use you to reach the next generation.

_____

_____

_____

_____

_____

_____

_____

_____

_____

2. Think about weaknesses and strengths. What strengths has the Lord given to you that you could use to reach others? But God doesn't just use your strengths; in his wisdom, he can also use your weaknesses, if you're open to him using them for his good. How can your weaknesses be used to relate to others and be real with them, to help guide them to their Savior?

_____

_____

_____

_____

_____

_____

_____

_____

_____

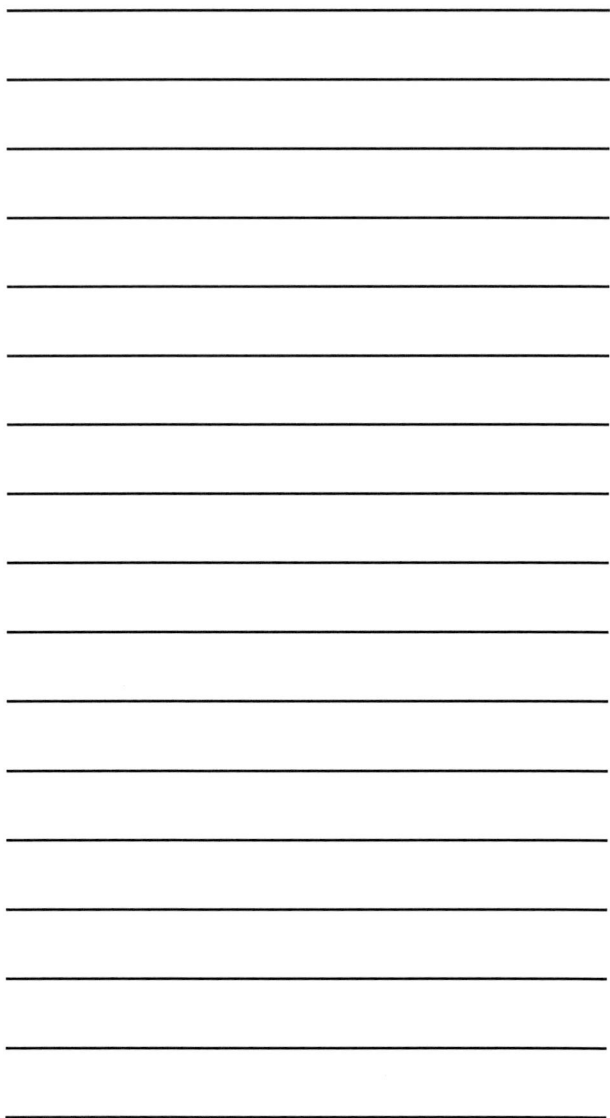

Even When Church Hurts

What will you do when I sin against you? I'm not planning on it or anything, but I need you to think about that question. What will you do when I sin against you? You see, I love being a pastor. And I hope you love being a part of this ministry—whether it's a church member or as a viewer of *Time of Grace* or as a reader of books like this one. I want us to grow in faith together for years to come. Which is why I didn't ask *if* but *when*. What will you do *when* I sin against you?

I was doing the math the other day. I speak about 5,000 words in an average sermon. That's about 250,000 sermon words a year. Add to that all the pre-church words and post-church words and counseling words and emailed words and texted words and written words and grab-coffee words and I speak millions of words to you. So what are the odds that one or two or ten of those words will be rude? or proud? or unfair? or exaggerated? or selfish? or just sinful? The odds are, sooner or later, I will sin against you.

I'm asking because I've heard the stories that separate generations from Jesus. Every year, I sit down with a whole bunch of different people and say, "Tell me your story. With God. With church." And people do. "Well, I used to go to church as a kid, but then the pastor said this thing to my mom and . . ." "I got pregnant and I just, I don't know, felt like people were judging me, so I left." "I went to the Bible study for a while, but then she said . . . and I know it sounds dumb but I felt so . . ." So often, it was one word, one disagreement, one decision, one look, one feeling, one sin that caused the separation. And people go years, even more, without a regular connection to Jesus' words or Jesus' people.

This book is about connecting the next generation to Jesus. The grade-schoolers and teenagers and college kids and young adults. And if that's you, you need to be prepared to answer that question. In fact, you have more sins that will happen against you coming your way than the old folks reading this. So, you need to think carefully. What will you do when we sin against you? But that question also matters for you boomers and Gen Xers and millennials too.

You're the friends, the older brothers, the parents, the uncles, the coworkers, the neighbors of the next generation. If we lose you, we lose them too. If you lose your roots in Jesus, we also lose the seeds that

What will you do when they sin against you?

were in your fruit, the next trees God wanted to grow. So, this question is for us all: What will you do when they sin against you?

Jesus wants to answer that question. Jesus knew, better than anybody, the garbage that would happen in the family of God. And Jesus cared, more than anybody, about the people who would be hurt because of it. And that's why Jesus told us exactly what to do. In chapter 1 I shared Jesus' words from Matthew chapter 18 about the next generation. "I love the kids," Jesus said. "Don't sin against the kids," Jesus warned. "Even if just one of them wanders, your Father is not willing that one of these little ones be lost." That's what Jesus said in Matthew 18:14. But do you know what he said in verse 15? The very next words? He said what to do when someone sins against you!

"If your brother or sister sins, go and point out their fault, just between the two of you. If they listen to you, you have won them over" (Matthew 18:15). This is important stuff! If your brother or sister sins, if someone in the church sins against you, what do you do? You go. Don't skip Sunday. Don't wait for that person to apologize. You go. You talk. Unless it's something atrocious—abuse, assault, that's a different story that requires a different step— you go. *You go and show.*

Do you know why this is so agonizing? Because it's effective! Because the devil knows the power of forgiveness. So, he lies. A lot. "She wouldn't listen anyway. He doesn't care. You know how they are. Don't waste your time." The devil has a PhD in exaggerations and worst possible constructions. "He said that because he's just in it for himself." "You see, they're hypocrites like all the rest." Oh, the devil lies because he's seen when people forgive. That one step clears up so many misunderstandings, builds so much empathy, offers the "I'm sorrys" and "I forgive yous" that increase our love for one another. It's a hard but a holy conversation.

The other day, a Christian took this step with me. I said something stupid. Not my intention, but looking back it was stupid. Insensitive. Proud. Sinful. So he emailed me. Called me out. Told me how wrong I was. His words were hard to read, but I was glad he reached out because I got to email him back, to own it, to confess what an idiot I had been. And do you know what happened? He forgave me. Said my email helped him see the situation in a new light—even pastors sin. He promised he would move on and not bring it up again. We reconciled. God blessed the "go and show" step Jesus gave.

That's what you do when they sin against you. Before the lies lock the door to that conversation, you go. So can I ask, do you need to go? Is there some tension, some awkwardness, someone you've been thinking about? If so, go. Get out your phone right now if you have to. Put this book down if you need to. This matters so much to Jesus. It will be awkward for you, hard to hear for them, but it leads to the best possible place. Forgiveness, unity, reconciliation, love.

Okay, but what if it doesn't work? What if they don't listen? Jesus is glad you asked.

Matthew 18:16 says, **"But if they will not listen, take one or two others along, so that 'every matter may be established by the testimony of two or three witnesses.'"** I love Jesus so much. He refuses to let sin spoil his family. He has no time for get-over-it, under-the-carpet cover-up in his church. He has no asterisks and no exceptions for the lead pastors, the big givers, or the long-time members. If I sin, if they sin, we gotta deal with it. We gotta talk. Sin is like cancer, and this is the chemo that kills it. Bring a brother, a sister, and deal with sin together. *Go and show (but not solo).*

Picture it like this. You and I are side by side, worshiping Jesus together. But then I sin, and I turn away from Jesus and from you and think of myself only. When that happens, it's very tempting for you to run, to give up, to bail on the church, to sin in your own way. But Jesus says, "No. Go. So you turn toward me, and you try to help me see the sin. Hopefully I do, and we have a better fellowship than ever before. But if I don't, bring someone with you. That witness will either tell me I really sinned, this is really serious, or they'll tell you, "You know what? I don't think this is a sin. It's a misunderstanding. A difference of opinion. He's okay. You're okay. Go in peace." And we humbly go back to worshiping Jesus together. That's what you do when they sin against you.

Now, I won't go through the other steps Jesus gave. You can read them another time if you'd like, but I'll show you the reaction one man had to Jesus' answer to our question: **"Then Peter came to Jesus and asked, 'Lord, how many times shall I forgive my brother or sister who sins against me? Up to seven times?' Jesus answered, 'I tell you, not seven times, but seventy-seven times'"** (Matthew 18:21,22). What?! 77 times?! If every Sunday for a year and a half they sin against me, I still forgive?! If they listen, repent, try again, I don't bail but bear with them? Again and then again and then again? "Yup," Jesus said. "In my church, it's not one strike and you're out. It's 77 strikes and you keep swinging." Here's how one of Jesus' later followers said it, **"Bear with each other and forgive one another if any of you has a grievance against someone. Forgive as the Lord forgave you"** (Colossians 3:13). Yes, there will be sin.

Yes, you will be grieved. So forgive. Bear with each other. *When church hurts, don't bail on but bear with.*

Okay, wow. That sounds . . . hard. Humbling and really hard. Why would we? Many people church hop, church shop, or church drop, so why would you be different? Let me give you two reasons.

Forgive. Bear with each other.

First, because the best relationships bear with. If you've ever dated someone or gotten married or had a lifelong friend, you know that you need a lot of strikes to get to something good. You can bail after every sin if you want, but you'll end up single, friendless, and completely alone. Friendship—your tribe, your crew, your guys—requires forgiveness. A great marriage requires 77 forgives a month! But if we work through it, if we bear with it, how good is it? The most fruitful trees have been through a lot of storms. The most fruitful Christians have been through a lot of sins. That's what can happen at church. We can be known and be loved. We can bear with one another. It could be the best.

But there's a second, better reason not to

bail. The reason Jesus gives in Matthew chapter 18. While Peter's brain did the 77x math, Jesus told a story about a man who owed a king 10,000 bags of gold. Some scholars calculate that to be 200,000 years of work! An absurd debt that the man couldn't pay. So, what did the king do? He took pity on him. He canceled the debt. He let him go.

What was Jesus' point? That even if they hurt you 77 times, you've hurt God 10,000 times more. Before you run for the door, check the record of your sins. Every choice you made for your glory and not his. Every word you spoke to express yourself no matter who got hurt. Every thought you thought that didn't trust God, didn't rely on God, didn't find peace in God. It would take 200,000 years of good works to work that off. So, what did King Jesus do? He didn't bail on you. He bore with you. A famous prophecy about Jesus said, **"He poured out his life unto death, and was numbered with the transgressors. For he bore the sin of many"** (Isaiah 53:12). Jesus bore the sins of many, and he bore our many sins. He put them on his shoulders and carried them to the cross. He didn't run away. He rescued us. He went through the hard part to give us an easy yoke, went through hell to give us heaven, didn't count up but canceled the debt, and shed his blood to set us free.

Jesus didn't bail on you. And he won't. Because he wants something really good, a long-time life with you, an eternal life with you. So, his grace keeps going. His faithfulness is fresh every day. His mercy is new every morning. That's why we love Jesus, right? It's why we tell the next generation the praiseworthy deeds of the Lord. Why we so badly want our friends and kids and grandbabies to know Jesus, trust Jesus, seek Jesus. That reason, the unending forgiveness of God, is why we bear with one another. Why we forgive. Because he first forgave us. No one loves us like this. Jesus is the best because he didn't bail. You are blessed because he didn't bail.

His mercy is new every morning.

I don't know when sin will happen in your church next. I hope not soon. I pray not often. But when it does, we know what to do. Talk. Forgive. Bear with each other in the name of the Savior who bore with us.

Like one family from my church did for me. They gather around at church a lot and do life in groups and give their talents to bless us. They've made a lot of connections, made a lot of good friends. They're rooted in Jesus, and their little boy is growing up with a lot of Jesus. But that only happens because his mom knew what to do when I sinned against her. I said something clueless in a sermon (again) and didn't realize how hurtful my words were (again). And she could have bailed. But she didn't. She bore with me. We talked. She forgave. They stayed. They kept growing in Jesus. And now the next generation can too.

Study Guide

1. The church is full of sinners. Hurts will happen. Matthew 18:15 gives you the first step of what to do when someone sins against you. Before you post anything on social media or speak behind the offender's back, what should you do? Why is this so important, especially in this day and age of quick texts, misread emails, and free gossip?

_____

_____

_____

_____

_____

_____

_____

_____

2. Matthew 18:16 tells you that if the first step doesn't work, you should take one or two others along with you as witnesses. You should choose these people wisely (not just choosing friends whom you hope will take your side). What qualities should those witnesses have? What is the point of this second step?

_____

_____

_____

_____

_____

_____

_____

_____

_____

_____

_____

3. In light of the verses just prior to this section (Matthew 18:12-14), what is the purpose and goal of going and showing your brother or sister their sin? Why is the term *brother/sister* important in this context?

_____

_____

_____

_____

_____

_____

_____

_____

_____

_____

_____

4. Ephesians chapter 4 also gives some advice about living in unity with one another in the church body. Dig into this chapter and focus especially on verses 2-6, 11-16, and 25-32. How do these verses fit into the study of Matthew chapter 18? Again, what is the ultimate goal that we have as a body of believers? Why is it important that we keep Christ as our Head?

_____

_____

_____

_____

_____

_____

_____

_____

_____

_____

Prayer

Dear Lord, I come before you with a heavy load. I want so badly to reach the next generation and spread the news of Jesus to them. I know you want that too. Lord, sometimes situations at churches full of sinful people can drive people away from the church and away from you. Thankfully, in your wisdom, you gave us some excellent guidelines in your Word. Help me to take your words to heart so that I can live in unity with others as one body of Christ. Help me to continue to grow as a member of a congregation of believers so that your Word may be spread to all generations. Amen.

Journal

1. Explore the topic of forgiveness. How does it feel to be forgiven, and how does it feel to forgive others? Consider your debt to God that he wiped away, and consider a debt or grudge you might be holding against someone. God did not bail on you, but bore with you. How can you more closely follow God's example?

_____

_____

_____

_____

_____

_____

_____

_____

2. Conflict is uncomfortable. The devil knows that, and he works hard to sow those seeds of discord in the church and drive God's people apart. The more we learn to deal with healthy conflict resolution, as suggested in Matthew chapter 18, the more unified we can become as a body of believers. Journal about a time you had to deal with conflict and how it was resolved. How is that relationship now?

_____

_____

_____

_____

_____

_____

_____

_____

Conclusion

Brothers and sisters, our Father is not willing that even one of these little ones be lost. So, let's do whatever we can to look and love the one who wanders. Let's step up as fathers, mothers, neighbors, and even sinners to show the beauty and power of the grace of God. Let's forgive one another in Jesus' name, for the sake of ourselves, and for the sake of the next generation who so desperately needs Jesus. Let's leave no one behind.

Notes

1 Jean M. Twenge, PhD, *iGen: Why Today's Super-Connected Kids Are Growing Up Less Rebellious, More Tolerant, Less Happy—and Completely Unprepared for Adulthood—and What That Means for the Rest of Us* (New York: Atria Books, 2017), 3ff.

2 Twenge, *iGen*, 128.

3 http://www.city-data.com/city/Appleton-Wisconsin.html.

4 Twenge, *iGen*, 122.

About the Writer

Pastor Mike Novotny has served God's people in full-time ministry since 2007 in Madison and, most recently, at The CORE in Appleton, Wisconsin. He also serves as the lead speaker for Time of Grace, where he shares the good news about Jesus through television, print, and online platforms. Mike loves seeing people grasp the depth of God's amazing grace and unstoppable mercy. His wife continues to love him (despite plenty of reasons not to), and his two daughters open his eyes to the love of God for every Christian. When not talking about Jesus or dating his wife/girls, Mike loves playing soccer, running, and reading.

About Time of Grace

Time of Grace is an independent, donor-funded ministry that connects people to God's grace—his love, glory, and power—so they realize the temporary things of life don't satisfy. What brings satisfaction is knowing that because Jesus lived, died, and rose for all of us, we have access to the eternal God—right now and forever.

To discover more, please visit timeofgrace.org or call 800.661.3311.

Help share God's message of grace!

Every gift you give helps Time of Grace reach people around the world with the good news of Jesus. Your generosity and prayer support take the gospel of grace to others through our ministry outreach and help them experience a satisfied life as they see God all around them.

**Give today at timeofgrace.org/give
or by calling 800.661.3311.**

Thank you!